Stained Glass Techniques

Art Work in Fabric

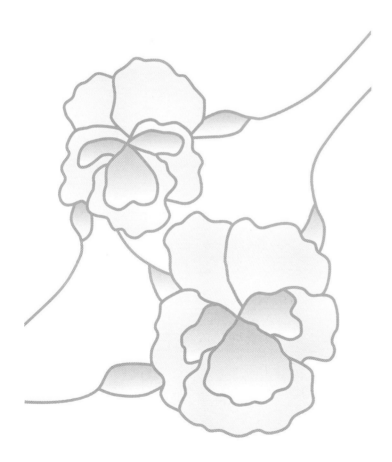

Marie Morel-Seroskie

Katie Lane Quilts

Dedication

This book is dedicated to my husband Jim. *Stained Glass Techniques* and Katie Lane Quilts would not exist as it does today without his support. There have been lots of on-our-own supper nights, un-ironed shirts, and dust bunnies learning the English language. Through all this, I have not heard a word of complaint. Thanks my Jim.

And thank you to my students who have encouraged me along the way. A special thanks also goes to Louise Barbash, Karen Burke, Donna Coon, Joan Herzog, Donna Rhodes, Kathy Stachowicz, and Vivian Summers. This book would have stayed in my computer without your help—forever lodged on the hard drive.

Published by Katie Lane Quilts
P.O. Box 560408
Orlando, FL 32856-0408

Photography: Jim Seroskie
Author and Designer: Marie Morel-Seroskie

Printed in the United States

Disclaimer: All suggestions in this book have been tried and tested in the classroom. Due to the vast number of variables in fabric and personal techniques, the author cannot guarantee the reader's results.

Every attempt has been made to properly credit the trademarks and brand names of items listed in this book. If we failed to do so, please let us hear from you.

Aileen's™ is a trademark of Aileen's, Division of Artis, Inc. Fray Check is a registered trademark of the Dritz® Corporation. Heirloom is a registered trademark of Hobbs Bonded Fibers. Hera™ Marker is a registered trademark of Clover Needlecraft Inc. Katie's Korners Radial Rule™ is a trademark of Katie Lane Quilts. Ott-Lite® is a registered trademark of Environmental Lighting Concepts. Inc. Quick Bias is a registered trademark of Clover Needlecraft Inc. Reynolds Freezer Paper Plastic Coated is a registered trademark of the Consumer Products Division, Reynolds Metal Company. Scallop Radial Rule™ is a trademark of Katie Lane Quilts. Schmetz is a brand name of Ferd. Schmetz GmbH., Germany. Stitch and Tear™ is a registered trademark of Freudenberg Nonwoven, Pellon® Division. Stitch Witchery is a registered trademark of Freudenberg Nonwoven, Pellon® Division. Thread-Wrap® is a registered trademark of Katie Lane Quilts. Wonder Thread is a registered trademark of the YLI Corporation.

ISBN 0-9667956-0-1

Contents

Introduction

Stained Glass Techniques—Art Work in Fabric, was written to take the mystery out of doing stained glass in fabric. I feel a sense of peace and true beauty while gazing at the beautiful stained glass in churches. Light radiating from behind the glass gives the work vibrance and life. Of course, we can't have light really radiating from behind fabric stained glass, but we can capture the beauty of the lines separating—and pulling together—the design and colors.

Working stained glass in fabric has some similarities to its glass counterpart. Fabric colors need to be picked for visual texture. We don't need leading to cover up and hold the sharp edges of glass together, but we do use bias strips to do the same for fabric.

My first stained glass project was a simple tulip. I had never done stained glass in fabric and didn't know how to do it, but one thing I knew, it would not be done by hand. My hand appliqué left a lot to be desired. It was painful to sew a hem by hand, let alone, a whole wall hanging.

So, after trial and error, it was settled. A fine blind-hem machine stitch was the way to go. It had the look of "hand appliqué" and that is what I was after.

Within the pages of this book, I will walk you step-by-step through a stained glass project—Pansies—from beginning to end. The pattern is included with the book. Suggestions will be made about simple techniques. I'll include ideas on such topics as choosing fabrics, color preferences for bias strips, and laying down the bias using various machine stitches. We'll even explore using a twin needle.

I encourage you to read through this book and, by the time you have finished, you will see how very easy it is to do stained glass—a true work of art in fabric.

Marie

Stained Glass Look

My hope is that you will find the pansy project in this book interesting and easy to do. My goal is to make doing stained glass "painless" and fun. I'll share different methods to achieve this look including the traditional make-your-own bias strips—but we'll do ours the easy way. I'll make every attempt to keep you from another "UFO".

Bias Pressing Bars

You may have purchased bias pressing bars—made from either metal or nylon—not knowing what they were for. Well, drag them out if you want to make your own bias strips. Making your own will take time, but the good news is the strips don't have to be turned!

It is important the bias pressing bars be thin. The metal are the thinnest but use caution—they conduct heat. The nylon bars can withstand the heat of an iron. If you press the bias strip with very thick plastic pressing bars, the fabric will tend to "roll". Check with your local quilt shop if you don't have any pressing bars. Complete directions for making your own bias strips will be given later. I encourage you to make one or two. The exercise will let you know if you want to continue making your own.

Pre-Made Bias Tape

There are several kinds of pre-made folded bias tapes on the market. There is a pre-folded bias tape available—Quick Bias by Clover. It is 100% cotton, ¼″ wide, and comes wound on a spool in many colors. Your local quilt shop should have it. This bias can be ironed on because it has a centered fusible backing. It can be ironed on by pressing in place so the raw edges of the pattern are covered. If the placement isn't correct, you can lift it up and press again. This fusible webbing is not meant to be permanent and needs to be sewn in place. In working with the Quick Bias—yes I gave in—I found that working with one piece at a time was best. I press on one strip and then sew it down before working on the next strip. When I tried to press three or four strips in a small area, some of the un-sewn bias would come detached as I machine sewed another piece. Even with the fusible web, it is easy to sew down either by machine or by hand because the fusible backing does not cover the edges of the bias fabric. According to the manufacturers directions, it is washable *after* being sewn in place.

Purchased shrink wrapped packaged bias from a discount retail store can also be used. You might want to test it for color fastness if the quilt is going to be washed. Wet a cotton swab and gently rub the bias to see if any color appears on the swab. My observation is this type of packaged bias tends to be light weight with a loosely woven fabric. It may be fine for a quick project, but I'd recommend a higher quality material for a "prized" quilt.

Grosgrain Ribbon

Some of my students confessed to using grosgrain black ribbon rather than making their own bias. The only drawback was that curves were not smooth due to the lack of bias in the ribbon. Grosgrain ribbon comes in a variety of widths and colors which could be suitable for different projects as long as the design has nearly straight lines.

Satin Stitch

A good close machine satin stitch works very well. I have used this on miniature stained glass patterns and was pleased with the results. You need a good stabilizer under your work—such as Stitch 'n Tear—to keep the satin stitch even and "proud". Since the satin stitches are so close together, the Stitch 'n Tear easily tears away after sewing. Try various stitch widths until you find something pleasing to you. Cotton or rayon thread work well. In fact, rayon gives the work a nice sheen. There are a variety of colors to choose from should you not want to use black.

Choosing a Method

Before starting your main project, try some or all of the above suggestions. Take the time to write down your observations. What were the machine settings? What worked best for the satin stitch, needle size, thread used, etc.

Later, I'll discuss the various methods of sewing down the bias strips. I encourage you to try each one of them.

> Tip: Make samples from each suggestion. Then write down your observations. What worked best for you?

Basics

Now is a good time to remove the pattern from the center of the book. There are three basic parts to any stained glass pattern: the background fabric, the lettered pattern pieces, and the bias or "leading" strips. Each "leading" bias line is numbered and all pattern pieces are lettered.

Pansies Pattern

Note the word "Center" with an "X". That "X" marks the center of the entire pattern. Use this to place the pattern in the center of your background.

Bias strip #10 is one long continuous piece. The arrows indicate the suggested sewing sequence. When you come to the center intersection, raise the presser foot to skip over the bias strip and continue.

There is an arrow pointing to bias strip #9. The note indicates not to sew that part down until #12 is tucked under. If you forget, free the edge of bias strip #9, snip with your scissors, and tuck #12 under.

Bias strip #24 is also one long piece. The arrows suggest the sewing sequence. Leave a little more of the strip sticking out than normal when you start. It is easier to trim it where you want as the other end gets back to the starting point. You may find it helpful to use a sharp object—like a long needle—to tuck and wrap the starting raw edge over the ending edge.

Pattern Pieces and Bias Strips

The pattern pieces are lettered. When transferring the pattern to either freezer paper or a fusible webbing, lettering each piece helps you keep track of all the pieces and where to place them. Lettering allows you to appliqué the pattern in sequence without the bias strips.

Each bias strip must be laid in a numbered sequence because you will always cover the raw edge of a previously sewn strip. Whatever stained glass pattern you have purchased, it will save you hours of frustration if you make sure each bias strip line is numbered in sequence so that any strip you sew covers any previously sewn strip it touches.

Transferring a pattern to fabric seems like a mystery to some quilters. I hope we can clear up some questions and simplify your quilt projects. There are various ways to transfer a pattern. I will address two methods—freezer paper and fusible web.

Transferring the Pattern with Freezer Paper

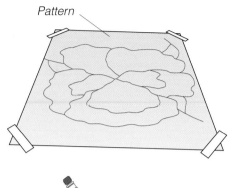
Pattern

Freezer paper may be purchased in your local grocery store. It can be found where the plastic bags and wax paper are kept. Freezer paper is only one of many products that has found application in the world of quilting. Personally, I prefer Reynolds freezer paper which proudly labels their paper for "Quilting and Other Crafts".

Freezer paper has a shiny side and a dull side. Drawing is done on the dull side. The *shiny side* is pressed to the *right side* of the fabric with a hot iron. The paper adheres to the fabric. If placement isn't correct, pull the freezer paper up, replace, and press with the iron. I have used these pattern pieces up to four times.

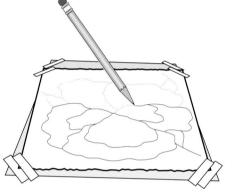
Freezer paper—shiny side down

If using freezer paper, it is not necessary to turn the original pattern over and redraw. Tape the pattern design down onto the table. Next, tape the freezer paper—*shinny side down*—over the pattern. Trace over the solid pattern lines and letter all the pattern pieces. It is not necessary to trace the "leading" lines shown on the pattern as dashed lines. These show you where to sew the bias strips.

If you have difficulty seeing the pattern, tape the pattern to a light source such as a window or light box.

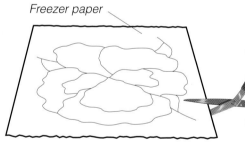
Freezer paper

Cut out each piece right on the drawn lines. *Do not add any seam allowance.* Finally, set these pieces aside, but don't forget to letter them.

Transferring the Pattern with Fusible Web

Fusible web has become a popular commodity in the quilt and craft world. It is basically a paper backed adhesive web sheet. Like freezer paper, it has a smooth side and a rough side. When the rough side is pressed to the *wrong side* of the fabric and the smooth paper removed, you now have another "glue" on the wrong side waiting to be fused to another piece of fabric.

Prior to using a fusible web, the original pattern needs to be redrawn. If you do not retrace, the result is a reversal of the pattern layout. The *exception* is a *symmetrical pattern* where one side is the exact mirror of the other.

Follow these steps:

- Turn the original pattern over and retrace the solid lines with a black felt tipped pen. Don't forget to letter the pattern pieces.

- Tape the retraced design down. Take a sheet of fusible web and place the rough side of the fusible webbing down on the pattern.

- Redraw the pattern on the smooth paper side lettering each piece as you go.

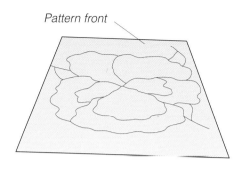

Pattern front

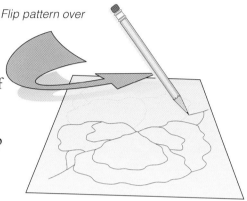

Flip pattern over

Trace pattern onto back
side to create a reverse image

Cut out each piece from the fusible web using a very sharp pair of scissors. *Do not add a seam allowance.* Caution is needed when you press the web to the background fabric because it can become detached from the paper. Make sure webbing and paper are right on top of one another. If not, your iron becomes "gummy" unless you use a teflon pressing cloth. Otherwise, just trace and cut another piece. Don't forget, the fusible web pattern pieces are pressed to the *wrong side* of your fabric.

Personally, I have worked with and like using Aileen's Hot Stitch Fusible Web. Make a sample before starting your project. Remember, hand quilting is nearly impossible if you use a fusible web. That may dictate which method you use.

Fabrics

There are so many good fabrics on the market today. Choose from those that resemble the real stained glass. Look for "mottled" or tone-on-tone fabrics—that is fabrics of a color but with muted intensities of that same color "splashed" in an all over asymmetrical design. Depending on the design, you can use more than one value of the same color.

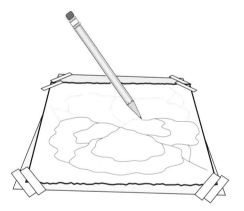

Fuzible web—rough side down

Hand dyed fabrics can truly enhance a pattern as can some of the beautiful batiks on the market. Some of these fabrics have several color runs to give you a wider choice.

Most quilters wash and press all their fabrics before starting a project. I must admit—confession time—I rarely wash my fabrics. However, in making my own bias strips, I will soak and wash black fabric.

Choosing a border fabric might be better done after the quilt top is finished. I find the quilt sometimes dictates what type of border—if any—would be better. Some stained glass fabric patterns are better left alone and just bound in the same color as the bias strips.

> Tip: Prepare all fabrics by steam pressing before transferring pattern pieces.

Pansies are such beautiful flowers and there are so many colored varieties available. I encourage you to search gardening books or your local garden center. Notice how the majority of pansies have darker centers than the outer leaves. Since this project is "Art Work In Fabric", I've taken liberties in choosing fabric colors with good "visual" textures.

The *background fabric* measures approximately 22″ x 26″. Fat quarters can be used for the pansies and leaves. It takes about seven yards of bias to do the whole wall hanging.

Choosing background or flower fabric first is your choice. Sometimes, I find the flower colors dictate what background is best and the same holds true in reverse. A "dull" background might just scream out for wild colors. Remember that in choosing fabrics, the bias strip will separate the colors. I am amazed how much a black bias defines colors and separates the background from flowers and leaves. Try placing a black bias strip between two similar fabrics to judge for yourself.

Test before making a final choice. Cut some of your favorite fabrics into approximately 4″ x 1½″ strips. Lay them out on various background fabrics. This helps you find a combination that works. You can go a step further. Butt the strips against one another and sew a black bias between each. This "separation" may give you a good idea how the fabrics work together. Try different bias strip colors too.

Getting Started

Now that we have transferred the pattern and cut our templates, let's start working with real fabric.

Background Fabric

Background fabric is just that, a background to help bring out the main pattern. Slip the pattern under your background fabric. Lightly retrace the pattern onto your fabric with a fabric marker. All you need are just some lines to indicate where to place your pattern fabric pieces.

You may need to use a light source if the design is not visible. Tape the design to a window or light box, place the background fabric on top, and trace the pattern lines with a fabric marker.

> Tip: Lay background fabric on widest part of the ironing board in preparation for securing your pattern pieces.

Transferring Freezer Paper Pieces

Place the freezer paper pattern pieces—*shiny side down*—on the *right side* of the fabric. When placing them down, choose interesting fabric design areas. Look for the darks and lights making good use of them for the particular design.

For example, the inside of a flower petal would look good if it were darker in value than the outside of the petal. It gives the flower more visual depth. You may want to work with only one or just a few pattern pieces at a time before pressing them down.

When the paper pattern is in place, press it down with a hot iron. The freezer paper will adhere to the fabric. Cut out the fabric following the freezer paper design. *Do not add any seam allowance.*

Place each cut pattern piece back on the main pattern until you are ready to continue. This helps keep track of all the pieces. There is nothing like loosing part of the fabric design only to find it months later behind the cutting table with attached fuzzies.

Securing Fabric Pattern Pieces

Carefully peel the freezer paper away from the fabric. Place the fabric pieces on the background following the pattern design. Make

Pattern fabric—right side up

Freezer paper pattern pieces—shiny side down

Press and cut

Background fabric
Pattern fabric pieces

Attach cut pieces to background fabric

sure the fabric pieces are butted up against one another. It will be difficult to cover a large gap with a ¼″ wide bias strip. Once all the pieces are butted against one another, you're ready to secure them to the background fabric. Here are some options for securing the fabric design pieces to the background.

- Pin and then baste the pieces to the background. The stitches can be removed later.

- Place small pieces of Stitch Witchery from a roll under the fabric pieces. Press with an iron.

- Pin in place using very fine appliqué pins. If sewing by hand, this may not be a good idea.

- Machine zigzag the pieces in place. Use a stabilizer on the back such as tracing paper. It is easy to tear-away or use tissue wrapping paper.

- Use an adhesive spray for a temporary bond. Spray either outdoors or in a well ventilated area. Spray more if it doesn't adhere.

Transferring Fusible Web Pattern Pieces

Remember, when using fusible web, retrace the original pattern onto the back side of the pattern.

Make sure all fabrics are facing you *wrong side up*. Place the fusible web pattern pieces with the *rough side down* onto the *wrong side* of the fabric. Press the web pieces following the manufacturers directions.

Cut out each pattern piece following the paper outline using a good sharp pair of fabric scissors. Leave the paper intact. Lay each cut piece on the original matching the letters—right side of the fabric facing up.

Take one pattern fabric design piece at a time and peel off the paper. Notice how the un-peeled side has a tacky feel to it and has no problem staying put on the background fabric. Just make sure the right side of the pattern pieces are facing you. Once all the pieces are in place and nicely butted against one another—meaning all raw edges are touching—press again following the manufacturers directions.

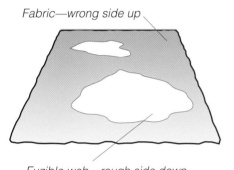

Fabric—wrong side up

Fuzible web—rough side down

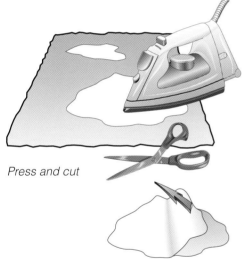

Press and cut

Peel web from pattern fabric

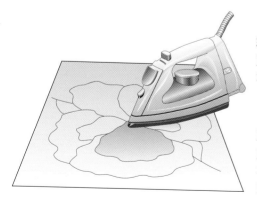

Place pattern fabric—right side up—on background and press

Bias Strips

Making your own bias strips is an option. It is a good rainy afternoon project. The strips can be precut all at one time. Another afternoon can be set aside for sewing, trimming, and pressing. Before you know it, a big stash will be done and just waiting for your next stained glass project.

Bias Strip Fabric

Choosing a color for the bias strips is a matter of preference. I prefer black as you can see from the color photos. It sets the colors apart from one another and makes a dramatic statement against the background fabric.

Other options might be gray, light brown, or whatever suits you and the project you are working on.

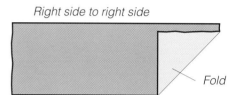

Right side to right side

Fold

Making Your Own

Choosing to make your own will take time but it allows you to make bias strips in many colors and even make them using prints. The method described below is simple. Best of all, there is no need to turn the strips inside out! Try making a few sample bias strips.

> Tip: Use caution when using the metal pressing bars—
> they get very hot. Nylon pressing bars do not get
> as hot but can still get very warm. In any event,
> use caution.

Take a piece of any fabric you have on hand not less than a fat quarter and press it.

Cut off fold

Bias strips are cut to the dimension necessary for the particular bias bar you are using. Follow the manufacturers directions. I chose to use a small nylon bias bar which makes ¼″ wide strips. The cut width of the bias strip for this small bar is 1″ wide. These bias bars are for *pressing* and not for sewing.

A rotary cutter, mat, and good acrylic ruler make cutting go fast. Remember, you are working with bias edges. We are tempted to smooth out our fabrics, but this can stretch the fabric out of shape. Be gentle.

- Lay out the fabric on your cutting board, with the selvage at the top and bottom. Take the bottom right hand corner and

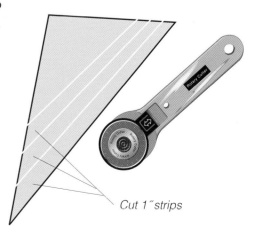

Cut 1″ strips

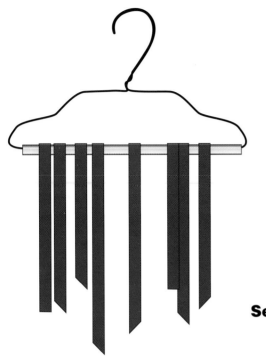

draw the fabric up. This forms a triangle as illustrated.

• Cut off the excess fabric while keeping the folded triangle.

• Leave the fabric doubled. Cut off the fold from the fabric triangle.

• Measure the width you need and cut the strips with a rotary cutter. Keep cutting the strips until you have no fabric left.

Tip: Layer the cut bias strips on a hanger wound with wide strips of muslin until you are ready to sew. This helps keep the wrinkles out. The muslin keeps them from slipping off the hanger.

Sewing Bias Strips

Thread your sewing machine with white thread both on top and in the bobbin. This helps save your eyes and makes for fewer mistakes when trimming. Set the stitch length from 12 to 14 stitches per inch. These strips will be cut and recut. Using a longer stitch length may make the seam weak.

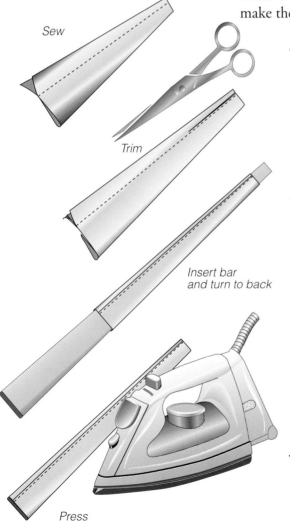

Sew

Trim

Insert bar and turn to back

Press

• Fold the strips in half—lengthwise—*right side out*. Sew ¼″ away from the double folded edge. After sewing one, insert the bias bar. Now is the time to make any adjustments. Speed sew the rest of the strips. In other words, don't start, stop, and then cut the threads after each strip is sewn. Get the next strip ready to follow behind the one already sewn.

• Trim the fabric to about ¹⁄₁₆″ away from the seam. Now you can see why it is important to use white thread.

• Insert the pressing bar into the sewn tube. Turn the seam allowance slightly off center on the flat side of the bar.

• Set the seam by pressing with a steam iron on a cotton setting. Work the bar through the tube. Press the fabric again after it passes through the bar.

• When you have a few strips pressed, line them up on the ironing board, spritz with either water or light starch, and press again. This helps make the edges crisp.

Tip: Soak and wash black fabric before using. Dry and press with a hot steam iron.

Curves and Miters

There are some basic sewing techniques that need to be addressed when sewing a bias strip. Bias strips allow for stretching. They can be sewn in a somewhat tight curve because of the "stretchiness" of the bias.

If you are using the Clover Quick Bias, you will notice it is fairly elastic. As you are stretching and pressing it around a tight curve or circle, the outside may want to lift up. Pinning it in place helps until you can sew it down.

I really "blap" the iron down with steam. I find it relaxes the bias and will do just about anything I want it to do. But a word of caution. Burnt blotches may occur if you leave the iron on fabric too long.

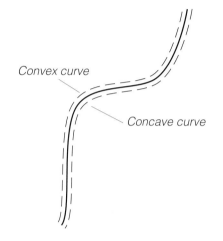

Convex curve

Concave curve

Concave and Convex Curves

A curved bias strip includes both an inside concave curve and an outside convex curve. When sewing down a bias strip, sew the *inside* of the curve first. After the inside curve is sewn down, you can push the un-sewn outside bias down and stitch in place. If you sew the outside curve first, the inside bias tends to pucker and gather.

Mitered Bias

Forty five degree miters are useful when going around sharp pattern pieces such as the tips of leaves or a sharp inside "V" shape. It is like putting a mitered binding on a quilt top. The same principles are used.

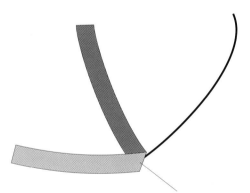

Fold back onto itself

Pin the bias in place before sewing it down making sure the miter is good and sharp. I use a makeshift stiletto—very long needle—to manipulate the fabric until a good 45° angle is achieved.

This method is not used in the pattern but it is a tip worth knowing.

Slight Curved Bias

Wavy pattern pieces like the pansy are simple to follow. Make good use of the bias by pushing and shoving the strip into place just before you either press, sew, or pin down. There is no need to sew the inside curves first if the curves are gentle.

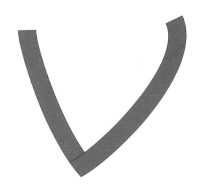

Completed mitre

Placing Bias Strips

Be sure to follow the numbered sequence for the bias strips in the pansy pattern. Some patterns don't come with the order numbered, so you will need to do this yourself.

Take a bias strip and cut a piece approximately ¼″ longer on each end of the pattern piece to be covered. This extra length allows for trimming at an angle in line with the pattern piece.

Center the bias strip so there is an even amount covering the raw edges of the pattern design and the ¼″ on each end evenly distributed. Sew the bias.

Sewing Bias Strips by Hand

Use a very fine black thread if you are going to sew the bias down by hand. Using a cotton covered polyester thread is not suggested. Cotton "marries" cotton. That fine single strand of plastic polyester tends to stand away from the cotton bias strip. Remember, a good 100% cotton or silk thread does a super job in fine hand appliqué.

I won't go into the subject of hand appliqué. There are many excellent books available on the subject.

Stabilizer

A stabilizer is important when sewing the bias strips by machine. It is nothing other than some sort of sheet that goes under your work. Put a stabilizer such as tracing paper or tissue paper under the background before you sew down the bias. This is especially important when sewing a bias strip alone on the background fabric. Try ironing on a sheet of freezer paper to the back for a stabilizer. Whatever you use, make sure it can be easily removed.

Center the bias strip

Fabrics

ckground Fabrics

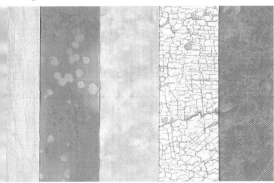

Background fabric should not dominate but rather lend itself to the design. Some of the samples range from dark to light and others are a tone-on-tone fabric.

Flower and Leaf Fabrics

Flower and leaf fabrics show the visual effect of light and dark coming through as it would in real stained glass.

Flower fabric in the left picture is of all one hand dyed piece. Pansy fabric in the two right pictures come from two sources. In either case, the background enhances the pansies.

Stitches

Blind-hem Stitch

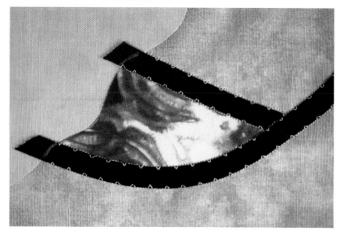

The blind-hem stitch has the look of hand appliqué in the sense that it is almost invisible. Use either clear or smoky nylon thread depending on the background fabric. Shown with white thread to emphasize the stitch.

Satin Stitch

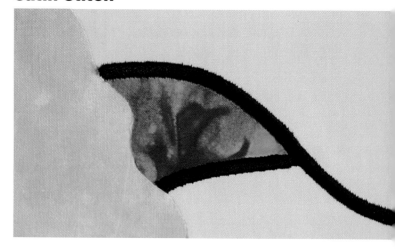

The satin stitch achieves the stained glass look and works well on small designs or miniature quilts. Satin stitches are good for tight curves where a bias strip may not fit and lie flat. Place a stabilizer under the background fabric for best results.

Zigzag Stitch

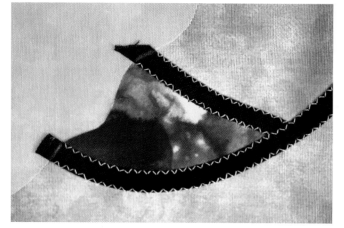

The zigzag stitch "zigs" on the background fabric and "zags" on the bias strip. This stitch is an alternative to the blind-hem stitch for sewing machines that cannot be adjusted for the smaller length and width of the blind-hem stitch. Using "invisible" nylon thread makes this an easy project. Shown with white thread to emphasize the stitch.

vin Needle

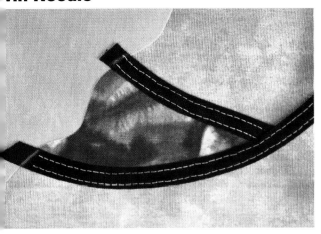

A twin needle makes for a fast project because both edges are sewn at the same time. Check your machine manual for directions. The bobbin thread on the back takes on the look of a zag stitch. Shown with white thread to emphasize the stitch.

Grosgrain Ribbon

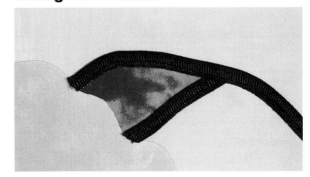

Grosgrain ribbon comes in a variety of colors and widths and is an alternative to purchasing or to making your own bias. It does not have any "give" but may be useful for more straight angular lines. The photo shows how it worked on a slight curve with minimum wrinkling using a twin needle.

Marking the Bias Strips

After sewing the bias strip, mark it with a fabric marker following the pattern design.

Trimming the Bias Strips

Trim the bias even with the pattern design to eliminate problems when placing the next overlaping bias strip.

Stained Glass Pansies I

Completed in 1998 by the author—20 ¾″ x 25 ¾″

Fabrics are 100% cotton. Machine appliquéd using a blind-hem stitch and machine quilted using variegated rayon and clear nylon thread.

Stained Glass Pansies II

Completed in 1998 by the author—24 ½″ x 28″

The background fabric gives the appearance of cracked glass. The border is the same as the leaf fabrics separated by a ¼″ black strip. All are 100% cotton.

Stained Glass Pansies III

Completed in 1998—22″ x 24 ¼″

The pansies are hand dyed 100% cotton fabric. The leaves are batiks and also 100% cotton. The bottom scallop treatment was achieved by using the Scallop Radial Rule.

Machine Stitches

Sewing machines offer quilters a wide range of stitches today. There are a number of methods available to sew down the bias strips. I'll show you three that I like. You may find others and I encourage you to experiment.

The Machine

There is nothing like sewing on your machine and all is going well until you discover the last two miles of sewing were all done without the help of the bobbin thread! It might be a good idea to fill a few bobbins before starting, and while you're at it, change the needle too. Those old dull needles can be used to hang light weight pictures.

How long has it been since you've cleaned your machine? Lots of lint loves to live in and around the bobbin case. If the vacuum cleaner is in the sewing room vicinity—which isn't too often—I use a long thin attachment and go over every single opening in my machine to pull out any dust, threads, and lint that gets lodged. I prefer not to use a can of air to blow it out. Some of that lint can be pushed further back only to collect and cause problems down the road.

Good lighting is important when working with black bias strips especially if you have a dark fabric for the flower. High contrast fabrics are easy to see but similar darks are difficult. I use an Ott-Lite and find it safe, cool, and bright.

Machine feet were mentioned before but it needs to be said again. Using an open toe foot gives you an eyeball view of where you are sewing and whether or not the raw edges are being covered. If you have a metal slotted foot, it will be more difficult to see where you're going. A clear embroidery foot works. Because you have a raised fabric in the bias strip, any of those feet have a groove that nestles over the bias strip. Check your sewing machine manual for foot options.

Blind-hem Stitch

My favorite technique is the blind-hem stitch. The blind-hem stitch is just that, difficult to see and has the look of hand appliqué. Thread your machine with clear nylon or smoky invisible thread. The bobbin thread should be the same color as your background fabric. One hundred percent two ply fine cotton is a good choice.

You could also use clear nylon thread for the bobbin. Wind the nylon on the bobbin at a very *slow* speed. Most of us tend to go too fast when winding a bobbin. Clear nylon thread stretches when being wound very fast. When placed back in its case, the thread will *relax* as you sew. It gets all scrunched up and wound around the bobbin case making a big mess. From my observations, there are also some machines that just don't like nylon thread either on top or in the bobbin. Do a test sample with your machine before you begin!

Tip: Use an open toe foot for all the suggested ways of sewing down the bias strips. It helps you see where you're going with no obstruction!

Set your machine for the blind-hem stitch. Your sewing machine manual will tell you how. Try sewing a piece of bias strip to scrap fabric before starting your wall hanging. Keep the needle for the straight stitches right next to the bias strip. Let the needle just *kiss* the bias as it sews the straight stitch. You'll notice there will be three or four straight stitches for every one stitch to the side. That stitch to the side is what "grabs" the bias strip and holds it in place. If your stitch length is too long, shorten the length. If the stitch width—the "grabber"—is too wide, adjust the width to make it narrower. Having said that, there are some sewing machines that will not allow you to tweak the settings. The stitch will only do what the machine was built to do. Don't give up if your machine will not do this stitch satisfactorily. There is another option—the zigzag stitch.

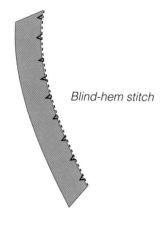

Blind-hem stitch

Zigzag Stitch

A zigzag stitch works well. The needle will "zig" on the background fabric and "zag" on the bias strip. Pick a zigzag stitch that is relatively small. You are attempting to mimic the look of a hand appliqué piece. Again, your machine may be preset and you cannot make the stitch length any shorter nor the width any narrower. What's a quilter to do! Maybe someone will buy you a new machine for your birthday! All right, if that doesn't happen, you can always try another option—a twin needle.

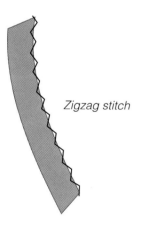

Zigzag stitch

Twin Needles

Twin needles allow you to sew down both sides of the bias at one time. Schmetz has an excellent assortment of twin needles. I suggest the 3,0/90 for ¼″ bias strips. You will notice there is one shaft that fits into the needle holder with two evenly spaced needles on either side of the shaft. Most machines are equipped to use a twin needle. Check your machine manual for placement of both spools of thread. On some of my samples, I used 100% fine cotton thread in each

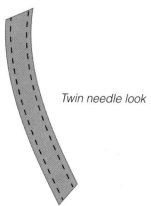

Twin needle look

needle and a fine black lingerie thread in the bobbin. The bobbin thread leaves a zigzag design on the back. It doesn't matter because it will not show once you have your quilt layered.

Trimming

It helps to mark the end of the bias strip at the same angle as the pattern piece that lie underneath. This can be done after you begin to sew the bias down. It will help to make an accurate cut.

Trim the edges of the bias after you have sewn at least one side and not before. Trim at the same angle as the pattern design. Not to do so can result in some exposed raw edges of both bias and pattern pieces. You know how much we quilters like to rip things out!

Bobbin Thread

Should the bobbin thread show on the top of your work, loosen the upper tension to a lower number. Most of our machines have the bobbin tension set anywhere between four and six. In sewing the bias, I keep mine at about a three.

Try this on scrap fabric of the same colors used in the quilt. Sew only the inside flower and leaf bias with black thread in the bobbin. Next, swap out the bobbin thread for a lighter color. Finally, sew down the outside bias edge against the lighter colored background.

Tip: Try all of the suggested stitches on scrap fabric before sewing your project. This will save you time in the end. Check the Trouble Shooting section in this book.

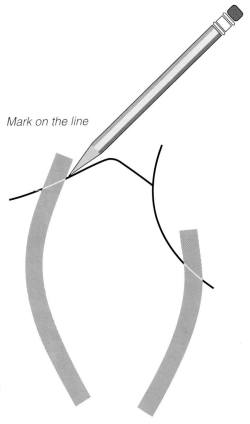

Mark on the line

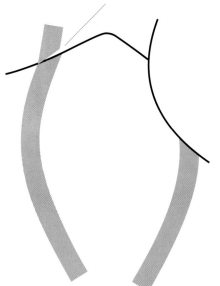

Trim bias at same angle as pattern line

Putting It Together

Let's look at some special features of our pansy design.

Squaring Your Quilt

We need to square up the quilt top before layering the backing and batting. You may have seen some quilts with "wings" or points on the corners. That quilt wasn't squared up. I use my husband's 90° carpenter's framing square for a large quilt . For smaller projects, I use my 16″ square.

I find it easier not to cut off the excess. I prefer to mark the squared up line and use that as a guide when applying the binding and trim later.

Borders

The color insert includes samples of pansies with and without a border and even one with a bottom scalloped edge. The black edging on Pansies I acts as a stained glass border and binding. Note the ¼″ black fabric separating the border of Pansies II and the addition of the black binding. This makes the pansy seem to float in the border.

Measure quilt at center in both directions

Measure the quilt through the center in both directions to find the correct length and width for a border. For a non-mitered border, sew border strips on each side of the quilt. Press the seam allowance to one side and sew on the border at the top and bottom. Then press.

Lay out your piece and try different fabrics folded in strips to simulate a border. Place them next to the quilt top. It becomes obvious when a fabric doesn't work.

Think about rounding the four corners, adding scallops, or anything else to add punch to your quilt top.

Marking the Quilt Top

Add left and right borders

Use a marker that can easily be washed or removed according to the manufacturers directions. Try any fabric marker first on a scrap to see how it reacts when you remove it.

There is a marker—the Hera Marker by Clover—which is a molded hard plastic that scores the fabric. In other words, if I want to make straight lines, I line up my ruler on the quilt top and run the Hera Marker right next to the ruler—much like you would a rotary cutter. A slight indentation of the fabric appears when the ruler is removed. These lines are the quilting lines and "disappear" once the quilting is done. There is nothing to remove. It can also be used for curves if the radius is not too tight.

Backing and Batting

There seems to be a trend in the quilt world to use a complimentary fabric for the backing. Plain muslin is being replaced by beautiful fabrics which in the past, we would have used for the main design. This would be rather expensive for a large quilt. Look in your stash and maybe there is a piece of fabric you bought in the past not knowing what it would be for. Cut the backing 1″ to 2″ wider all around than the quilt top. Then press.

Add top and bottom borders

The batt world today gives us so many choices, but it really comes down to what you like to use. My own preference is Hobbs Heirloom Cotton Batting. It has a ratio of 80% cotton and 20% polyester. If you are going to wash your quilt after it is quilted, it is better to soak this batting according to the manufacturers directions to prevent shrinking.

Place the backing—right side up—on top of the batting and cut the batting to the same size. Next, flip it over and lay the quilt top on top of the batting. If you are machine quilting, baste using safety pins or whatever method you normally use. Should you hand quilt, the traditional hand basting method works well. After quilting your pansies, you are ready for the binding.

Quilt top
Batting
Backing

Quilting by Machine

You might want to test different threads. Try the clear nylon and the smoky nylon. I prefer the YLI Wonder Thread in both the clear and the smoky. Should you be using a very light fabric, the smoky nylon just might show up more than you want.

Whatever you use, choose a good quality nylon rather than a spool that could double as fishing line. Heat test it with your iron. There are some clear nylons that may get brittle when pressed with a hot iron. You will probably have to press the entire top before layering the backing and batting. I press with a steam iron from the wrong side. Use a pressing cloth.

For bobbin thread, I use 100% cotton–60 weight–two ply. It is a fine thread and works well with the nylon. I'm able to get those two extra miles out of one bobbin because of its weight and ply.

Variegated rayon threads work well with flowers and leaves for machine quilting.

What design to quilt? There are some quilters who come to a halt on their project at this point. For stained glass, there is one consistent quilting form that I follow. I quilt on either side of all the bias strips. Rayon threads, the color of the flowers and leaves, was chosen for this project. Clear nylon was used on the background fabric along the bias.

Hand quilting any stained glass project may be difficult if you have used a fusible web because the bonded fabrics have a stiffness to them. However, you can use the stab stitch method. Try this on a scrap. Push the quilting needle *all the way through* the quilt to the back. Then bring the needle *all the way through* back up to the front. A combination of machine and hand stitching is perfectly acceptable.

Next, look at the flower petals and leaves. Make up vein lines in both. As for the background itself, try echo designs, cross hatch, meandering, or free form leaf designs.

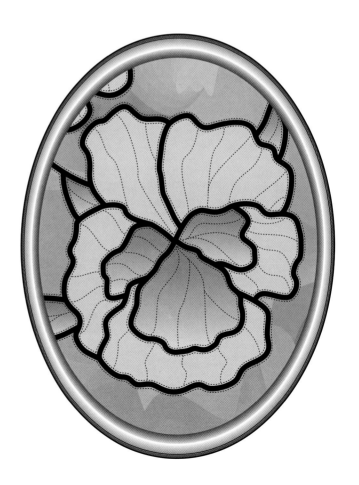

Finishing Touches

This is the time I really get excited—the end is in sight. And now is also the time to take special care to prevent another UFO from being birthed.

Mitered Binding

We're now ready to bind all around the outside edge of the quilt.

- For cross grain binding strips, measure the perimeter of the quilt top in inches. Divide by 40—forty is the selvage-to-selvage measurement in inches. Round this number up and you have the number of strips needed for the binding.

  For example, if the result after you divide is 3.5 (that's 3½), round up to the next number—4 in this case. How much fabric you need depends on how wide you cut the binding strips. I cut mine anywhere from 2″ to 2½″ wide. Should you decide on 2″ strips, you need 4 strips in this example at 2″ per strip. So you cut an 8″ piece of fabric—40″ wide.

- Sew the strips together on the bias. Trim and press the seam to one side. If you choose, you may instead press the seam open—your preference.

- Fold the starting end up to form a triangle, press, and trim to within ¼″ of the fold. Fold the bias lengthwise in half and press.

- Stitch the binding by machine, starting about one quarter of the way down from the top.

- Miter the four corners, trim the backing and batting even with the binding, and turn the binding to the back and slip-stitch in place.

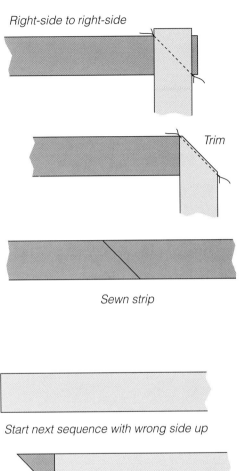

Right-side to right-side

Trim

Sewn strip

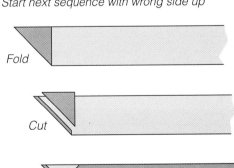

Start next sequence with wrong side up

Fold

Cut

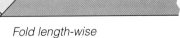

Fold length-wise

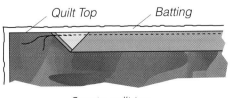

Quilt Top *Batting*

Sew to quilt top

Fold at corner

Fold again

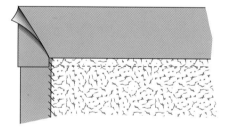

Butted Binding

There is an alternative method to binding a quilt that isn't seen as often as a continuous binding with mitered corners. A butted binding is similar to sewing borders on each side followed by the top and bottom.

- Cut four strips 2″—or more—wide on the cross grain— selvage-to-selvage. For a very large quilt, sew the strips together.

- Fold in half and press the entire length of the strip.

- Stitch a binding strip to each side of the quilt. Trim, turn back, and stitch by hand.

- Stitch the remaining strips on the top and bottom of the quilt. Make sure to have ½″ extra on each side to turn and cover the raw edge of the first binding strips. Turn the binding to the back and hand stitch.

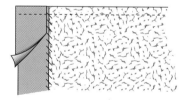

Stitch binding strip

Sew top and bottom strips

Turn strip up and over

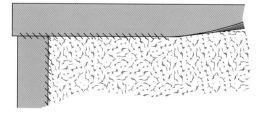

Stitch by hand

Making a Hanging Sleeve

There are various ways to attach a hanging sleeve on the back of a quilt. The purpose is to allow you to insert a rod or slat and hang the quilt.

- Cut a piece of fabric 8″ wide by the width of the quilt top. I tend to use the same fabric as the backing. Fold each end under about ¼″, press, fold again, and stitch.

- Fold the sleeve lengthwise, wrong side to wrong side, and sew a ¼″ seam allowance.

- Roll the sleeve tube so the seam is in the middle. Press the seam allowance open. It won't show once it is tacked down to the quilt top.

- Hand stitch along the top just below the binding.

- Roll the sleeve edge up so it is not quite even with the top edge of the binding and pin in place. Pin the bottom of the sleeve and tack down. The reason for "rolling" the sleeve up is to allow for some room so the inserted bar will not distort the quilt top.

For small wall hangings, you can use a yard stick or slat as the hanging rod. Cut the yard stick so that it is about ½″ short of each end of the quilt top. Drill a hole on each end, hammer the nails in the wall, and hang that beautiful top!

Tip: To make a sleeve, use left over fabric strips from your project.

Cut 8″ strip and finish ends

Fold lengthwise and sew

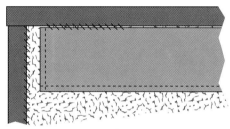

Hand stitch just below binding

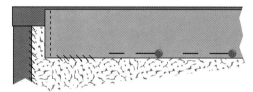

Pull sleeve edge up to edge of quilt, pin bottom of sleeve, and stitch

Binding Curves

Adding rounded corners or scallops to a quilt gives it a different look. Curved edges do need a binding cut on the bias so it can "stretch" around all those rounded edges.

Rounding Quilt Corners

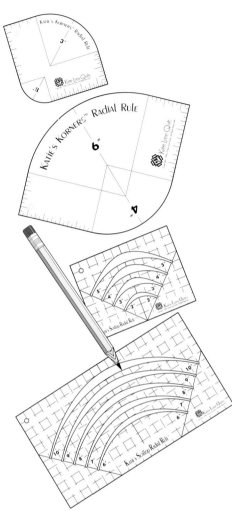

Rounding corners of a quilt can add interest and variety. It is necessary to square up the four corners of a quilt before rounding. Traditionally, quilters used plates, saucers, cups, and anything else that was round to mark the top. Making sure all four corners are exactly the same is quite a task.

Katie's Korners Radial Rule make this job a snap. These templates have a straight tangent edge on each side of a 90° arc. It takes no time to line up those tangents with the straight edges of the quilt corners and draw the radius. It's quick and accurate. They come in two sizes—for large and small quilts—with two radii on each.

Mark all four corners but do not cut just yet. The drawn line will be your guide for sewing on the binding. Should the fabric be cut now, there would be nothing but bias on all four corners. This makes for a very wavy quilt top. Once the binding is applied, trim the extra fabric, turn the binding to the back, and sew in place.

Tip: *It will be much easier if you trim the backing and batting after the binding is sewn.*

Scallops

Pansies III has a scalloped bottom. I would not have attempted doing this in the past. But now with the Scallop Radial Rule, it's a piece of chocolate cake.

For this quilt, I chose a single 3″ base line arc from the mini rule. Other more complex patterns are possible. I would choose something very simple for this project.

The Scallop Rule comes in two sizes with eight arcs available on the mini rule and another ten arcs available on the large rule. A book of tables is available if you need help with the math.

Making a Bias Tube

Just the thought of making a bias tube brings out the sweat on the brow of some quilters. It really isn't that difficult. I'll do my best to make it clear and understandable. The advantage of a bias tube is that there are only two seams with which to deal—unlike the many seams when bias strips are sewn together.

I suggest you make a miniature bias tube out of muslin before cutting into your good fabric. Cut a piece about 10″ square. However, before cutting, make pencil marks on one side to indicate the wrong side of the fabric.

- Cut the square in half on the diagonal with the right side facing you.

- Take the bottom triangle, flip it over top to bottom, and place it right side to right side on top of the other triangle. Stitch across ¼″ from the edge. Take your second muslin square— cut and sew.

- Open and press the seam allowance either to one side or open—your preference. Remember not to pull on the bias part of the fabric. Draw a line on the non-bias sides ¼″ from the edge.

- Draw the cutting lines from 2″ or more across the bias. Notice

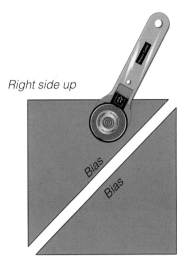

Right side up

Cut diagonal

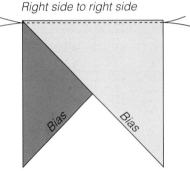

Right side to right side

Sew 1/4″ seam

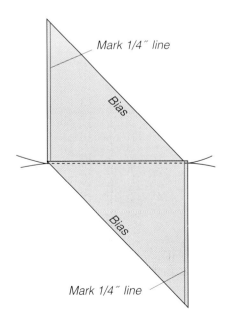

Mark 1/4″ line

Mark 1/4″ line

how these lines intersect the ¼″ line previously drawn. An "X" is made at that point. This "X" will save you time and a headache or two when you match those two non-bias edges. Don't worry if the last strip doesn't measure the same width as the others. Cut about 5″ into the first drawn bias line.

- Now comes the part where most quilters get confused—hang in there with me. If you had not cut on the first drawn line before sewing the two straight edges—A and B— you would be cutting out hoops. That first cut makes for an offset cylinder. When cut, you go around-and-around winding up with a pile of bias fabric.

  Note the placement of the two pins on side A and side B. One is on the first drawn line and the other pin is on the second line. Pin sides A and B together matching the two pins at the "X" points. Continue pinning at each "X" intersection.

- Sew across on the ¼″ line drawn on the straight non-bias edge. Use scissors to cut along the drawn lines.

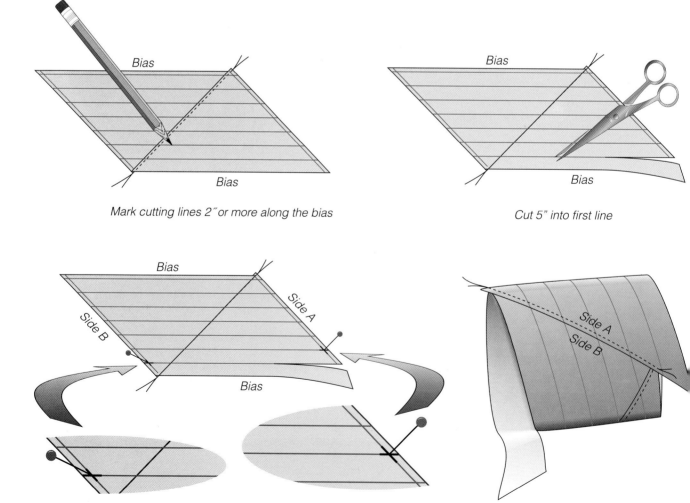

Mark cutting lines 2″ or more along the bias

Cut 5″ into first line

Trouble Shooting

I hope things have gone well for you, but few projects are perfect. Some problems can be avoided but for others—well "stuff just happens". Let's hope you don't need the following tips too much.

Bobbin Thread Shows on Bias Strips

Should your bobbin thread show on top of the bias strips making little "tick" marks, try lowering the number on the upper tension to about a three—low is loose—high is tight. If that doesn't work, try using clear nylon in the bobbin. When filling the bobbin with this type of thread, do it slowly to minimize stretching.

Bobbin Thread Shows on Pattern Pieces

If your background fabric is a light color, you should have a light colored thread in the bobbin. The flower piece may be dark and the bobbin threads are poking up and you are almost at "zero" on the upper tension. When this happens, I change my bobbin thread to a darker color to match the flower. This means the inside bias strips are sewn down first. Then you can tackle the outside bias changing the bobbin to the lighter color.

You might also consider using clear nylon in the bobbin to solve this problem. I urge you to practice on a scrap piece to see if you like the results. Remember to wind clear nylon thread on a bobbin at one mile per hour—not two hundred!

Forgotten Ends

Bias strip #12 is being stitched down and you realize #9 has been completely sewn down already. Not to worry. Clip a few threads and with a stiletto or other sharp object, nudge #12 in place.

Fraying Fabric

Some fabrics tend to fray more than others. Try a little bit of Fray Check on the edges of the fabric pieces. This is available in fabric shops.

Fusible Bias Strips

When using Clover's Quick Bias, I have found that if I press a large area at one time, the tape comes away from the fabric the more I handle it. Do one piece at a time to avoid this problem.

The fusible web does not interfere with machine sewing. The needle won't get "gummy" even when using a twin needle. The same is true if you are sewing by hand.

Gluing

Before using a fabric glue, make sure it doesn't leave a stain mark or residue on the fabric. I have used a regular glue stick to hold down some of the pieces with success.

Perhaps you have used an adhesive spray and the pattern pieces still separate from the background. Try spraying on more. It seems obvious, but I have been too timid with spray myself at times. More helps.

Missed Areas

You're done and you discover the raw edge of one of the fabrics wasn't covered by the bias strip. There are two ways to handle this. Take out the bias strip stitches that are in the effected area, move the bias, and resew. Or, if it isn't too bad, dip a tooth pick into some Fray Check and gently, "moosh" it in the fabric. It's sort of cheating, but believe me, it works!

Pinning

Pinning down the bias strips may help especially when you have a sharp inside curve or a mitered corner. There are times when you need to pin down the points of leaves and flower stems.

Notes

About the Author

Marie Morel-Seroskie was in the educational system as a teacher and administrator for about 20 years. She authored a children's book for Sadlier-Oxford in 1978. Having had an active teaching career and a Masters in Education, she shifted her enthusiastic approach to the world of quilting after being introduced to it while traveling in the early 1980's.

She started her own line of patterns under the name of Katie Lane Quilts in 1991. The first was a simple stained glass tulip. Other more complex projects have followed. To this day, most of her patterns are unique stained glass designs known for their graceful flowing lines and clear directions.

Marie's strength is the teaching of techniques using a style filled with good humor. She likes to give her students a solid foundation which they can use as a stepping stone for continued growth.

This is the first in a series of books with this one designed to ground you in her easy stained glass technique. She takes you through every step of making a stained glass pansy wall hanging, removes the mystery, and give you practical tips along the way.

Other Katie Lane Quilt products developed over the years have included Thread-Wrap, the Katie's Korners Radial Rule, and the Scallop Radial Rule. Each has been the product of a collaboration with Jim—her husband of 22 years.

Enjoy!